The X-bots are Coming ...

Anthony McGowan ✶ Jonatronix

OXFORD
UNIVERSITY PRESS

Previously ...

On the surface, Greenville is just like any other city. But deep beneath the NICE building, lies the secret base of NASTI. The head of NASTI, Dr X, is hatching an evil plan. There is just one problem, he has lost four very important watches – watches with shrinking powers – and he wants them back!

X2 SPY-CAM

Dr X knows that four children have his watches. They have been using them to shrink down to micro-size. Now, Dr X knows where the children's micro-den is and the children must decide what to do …

"So what!" shouted Tiger. "I'm not scared of Dr X."

Max, Cat, Ant and Tiger were in their micro-den, a hollowed out tree stump on the edge of the park. They were all looking worried, apart from Tiger.

"You don't get it," gasped Ant. "Dr X knows where our den is. His X-bot spies have been tracking us. And now he's got a whole army of X-bots!"

"Ant's right," said Max. "We have to find a new den. If Dr X catches us he'll get the watches. Then he'll have all the power he needs for his evil plans."

"I agree," said Cat.

The others were surprised because Cat hardly ever agreed with anyone about anything.

"What do you say, Tiger?" asked Max.

"But I really like it here," he whined. "It's my favourite place in the whole world!"

"We've no choice," said Cat. "It's move or be captured."

"Well … OK," Tiger finally agreed.

"Why don't we use your old toy castle?" said Max. "It could be our new, temporary base. After all, it was designed to keep baddies out."

"Great!" said Tiger, perking up. "I'll go and get it right now." Tiger loved his toy castle, but he was a bit too old to play with it. He was secretly pleased that he might be able to use it again. "OK, Tiger," said Max. "There's no time to lose!"

Tiger ran down the stairs and out of the micro-den. He checked that no one was looking and used his watch to grow back to normal size. Then he grabbed his skateboard and whizzed off home to find his castle. He hoped it was still in the box under his bed.

"We know where they are hiding," shouted
Dr X, "but they still have my watches!"
He thumped his fist on the desk.

"It's his fault," said Plug and Socket at the
same time, each pointing at the other.

"Quiet, you fools!" screamed Dr X. "It's time
to get serious. It's time for Plan 3!"

"Plan 3?" asked Plug. "I didn't realize there had been a Plan 1 or 2!"

"Plan X3," said Dr X, with an evil snigger.

"Huh?" said Socket. "What's that, boss?"

"Follow me," replied Dr X, "and I'll show you."

Dr X led Plug and Socket down a long corridor. They entered a room with a large window on the far wall. The window looked down on to a big factory floor, full of machinery.

The machines were making X-bots. There were heads without bodies, bodies without legs and legs without heads or bodies.

"You see?" said Dr X. "Now that my new X3 production line is up and running, I can make as many X-bots as I want. I don't need buffoons like you any more. Humans are so weak, so foolish, so silly. The X3-bots will not fail me. They are perfect!"

Plug and Socket looked at each other.

"So, what are we going to do?" whispered Plug.

"Well," said Socket, "I've always wanted to drive an ice-cream van."

"SILENCE!" screamed Dr X. "I have assigned you both to new duties. From now on you will wash the dishes in the kitchen. When you've finished that, you can tidy up my office and after that you will clean the NASTI toilets."

"Oh, no!" groaned Plug and Socket.

Oh, no!

Tiger soon returned with his old toy castle. It would make a perfect micro-hideout.

"Now all we need to do is find a very secret hiding place," said Max. "Any ideas?"

Cat and Ant shook their heads.

"I think I spotted somewhere," said Tiger, beaming brightly. "Follow me.

Tiger led the others across the park. He stopped by a huge, old oak tree and pointed up into the branches.

"There's no way Dr X will find us up there," said Tiger. "And even if he does, everyone knows that grown-ups are rubbish at climbing trees."

Only Ant looked unhappy. "I bet Dr X's new X-bots can climb trees," he said.

"So?" snorted Tiger. "We'll be able to see them coming from up there."

"Just like you saw that one coming to steal your watch that time," chuckled Cat.

Tiger blushed. The others had never let him forget the time he nearly lost his watch.

"What if the new X-bots can fly?" Ant pleaded. "We'll be trapped up there in the tree if they attack us."

"Hang on," said Tiger. "This is nothing to do with the X-bots, is it? You're scared of heights!"

"It's not the heights I'm afraid of," said Ant sheepishly. "It's falling from them."

"I don't care what you're afraid of," replied Tiger.

"Stop it, Tiger!" said Max firmly. "Ant's right. This isn't a good hiding place. We'll have to think of something else."

Max, Cat, Ant and Tiger all sat down under the tree. They watched an old lady feed a few ducks that were swimming in the nearby pond. There was an island in the middle of the pond. It was too small for a grown-up, or even a child to stand on, but it was perfect for ducks. A couple of them were waddling about on it.

Max had an idea.

"Ant," he said, gingerly. "You're not afraid of water are you?"

"Of course I'm not. I've got my swimming certificate."

"What about the rest of you?"

Cat and Tiger realized what Max was thinking.

"That is genius!" gasped Tiger.

"Yes, very clever," agreed Ant. "There's no room for an adult on the island, but it will be perfect for us as micro-kids. And the pond will act as a moat, which might just keep the X-bots away."

"Brilliant," said Tiger. "I always wanted a moat for my castle."

"How deep is the water?" asked Cat, looking concerned. She knew that water could be dangerous, even if you could swim.

"It's not that deep," replied Tiger. "I should know. I fell in it last year!"

That didn't surprise anyone. Tiger was always getting in to scrapes, even before they found the watches.

"Hang on a minute," said Cat. "Just how are we supposed to get to the island?" She did not like the idea of getting her trainers and trousers wet wading over to it.

Ant had an idea. He cycled away and came back ten minutes later, carrying a box.

The others gathered round as he opened it. Inside was a shiny red, remote-controlled speedboat. The children gasped.

"I got it last year for my birthday," said Ant, "but I never really played with it. I like my science set better."

"Sometimes," smiled Tiger, "I'm glad you're so weird."

Chapter 4 – The Island

"We need to attach the castle to the boat," said Max. He looked around.

With Tiger's help, Max made a raft out of some drinks cans and an old piece of wood he found nearby. They tied the castle to the raft then tied the raft to the speedboat. They were ready to go.

"Right," said Max. "One of us should stay normal size and drive the boat from here, while the others ride over to the island."

"Me, me, me!" shouted Tiger.

Max wasn't sure, but Tiger promised to be sensible.

"Ready?" asked Max.

Ant dropped Rover into the boat and Cat nodded. They checked no one was around. Then they turned the dials on their watches. They pushed the X and …

Cat gazed down at the water.

"Ant," she asked, in a worried voice, "is there anything nasty in there? Anything that might eat us when we're this size?"

"Well, there are dragonfly larvae that have huge jaws and the pond skaters can suck your juices out. But I'd only be worried if there's a pike in the pond."

"What's a pike?"

"It's a fish, but when we're this size, a pike might as well be a shark."

Cat gulped.

"So let's make sure we don't fall in," said Max.

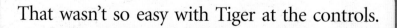

That wasn't so easy with Tiger at the controls.

Even though he'd promised to be sensible, Tiger drove the boat too quickly. It whizzed round the island making big waves. Everything got wet – including Cat's trainers!

Finally, Tiger steered the boat to the island and Max, Cat and Ant got out.

"Whose idea was it to let Tiger drive?" grumbled Cat.

"Sorry!" said Max.

They untied the raft and dragged it up on to the island. The boat spun round, making one final wave, then Tiger steered it back across the pond.

Tiger turned the dial on his watch. He pushed the X and …

It was more difficult to use the remote control now he was small.

The boat went this way and that. Waves crashed over the side of the boat.

Finally, he crashed into the island and landed face first in the smelly mud.

Back at NASTI, Dr X was looking at a large screen.

"So, those annoying kids have moved. They think they are so clever, but they're not clever enough. My X2 spy has found them already. And the X3 army is almost assembled."

Then Dr X laughed. And laughed. And laughed.

"What's so funny?" said Plug to Socket.

"Don't know," he replied.

X2 SPY-CAM

Chapter 6 – Ideas

The micro-friends dragged the castle to the middle of the island. They were tired, dirty and wet, but happy.

"This is a brilliant hiding place, Max," said Tiger. "Dr X will never find us here."

"I don't know," said Ant. "We still need to watch out for those X-bots."

"The X-bots are made of metal," replied Cat. "They'll sink in the pond, won't they?"

"Can we do a test with Rover?" asked Tiger. Rover beeped rapidly and his eyes flashed.

"You mean throw him in the water?" exclaimed Ant. "No way! He's one of us. Besides, they might have other ways of reaching us."

"OK," said Max. "We can't be sure that the X-bots won't be able to get on to the island. What we need are some extra defences."

"Wow!" exclaimed Tiger. "You mean like traps?"

"Exactly. Anyone got any ideas?"

"I'm sure there's lots of stuff in the micro-den we could use," said Ant.

So Max, Ant and Tiger headed back across the pond to the micro-den. Tiger found driving the speedboat much easier with Max to help him steer.

Cat stayed on the island with Rover, looking for other materials that would help build up the castle's defences.

Back at NASTI ...

"Step up production!
WE ATTACK IN ONE HOUR!"

Chapter 7 – Building the defences

Back on the island, the micro-friends began to build their traps and defences. Tiger was in charge of the first trap. He got the others to help him dig a large hole in the ground in front of the castle.

"It's a pit trap," he said, proudly. "It's what you'd use in the jungle to capture wild animals. We're going to put some twigs and grass on top of it. Any X-bot that walks over it will fall in!"

"But what's to stop them just climbing out again?" asked Cat.

"A-ha!" exclaimed Tiger. "That's where the second part of my idea comes in. We use this."

Tiger handed out pieces of bubblegum.

"Bubblegum?" asked Max.

Tiger groaned. "We need it for the trap," he explained. "Now, get chewing!"

They all chewed the bubblegum. Tiger blew a huge bubble, which burst, leaving a sticky, pink mess all over his face.

"I thought this was supposed to be serious chewing," Max scolded, "not just for fun."

"Spoilsport," said Tiger.

When the bubblegum was all sticky, Tiger told them to put it in the bottom of the hole.

"Oh, I get it," said Ant. "The X-bots will get stuck in the bubblegum. Very clever."

"I know," said Tiger, proudly.

"Right," said Max. "Now we're going to use one of those spoons to make a catapult, like they had in the Middle Ages."

Max did some calculations and made notes in his notebook. Then he did a drawing and stuck it on the castle wall. They all worked together, following his plan. They used the spoon, some ice-lolly sticks and several elastic bands to make the catapult.

"What's it going to fire?" asked Tiger.

"These," said Max, pointing to a pile of balloons.

"They won't do much damage!" said Cat.

"They will when they're full of water," replied Max.

"Cool," said Tiger. "Water balloons!"

They filled the balloons with water from the pond, tied knots in the end and put them next to the catapult. It was good fun moving the big balloons full of water. Tiger bounced up and down on one until it burst.

"Typical Tiger!" said Cat, but she couldn't help laughing.

Next it was Ant's turn. He had brought a strong magnet. There was a very springy tree branch hanging over the island. Together, the children pulled the branch down and tied it with some string to a big stone. Then they tied the magnet to the branch. Ant explained that the magnet would pull the X-bots towards it.

"What about you, Cat?" asked Ant. "Have you had any ideas?"

"Er …" she said. "I found some pieces of bread."

Tiger laughed at her. "How's that going to stop an army of X-bots?" he scoffed.

"Well, I thought it might help to keep the ducks on our side!" Cat said, looking hurt.

"Actually," said Max, "I think it's a good idea."

Chapter 8 – Bring me back my watches!

Back at NASTI, Dr X stood in front of the window looking out over the room where the X3 army were assembled. Hundreds of shiny black X-bots were looking up at him.

He spoke into a microphone.

"Now my beauties, the time has come. You have your orders. Do not disappoint me. Do not hurt the children but BRING ME BACK MY WATCHES!"

The army of X-bots marched through a secret door leading out of NASTI and into the drains. From there, the X-bots could reach any part of the city without being seen. Surely, nothing could stop them?

The micro-friends were getting ready to go home. They were very happy with their new, improved hideout. The castle was well camouflaged in the leaves and bushes of the island.

"I think we're going to be safe here," said Max.

"Definitely!" Tiger agreed.

"Wait," said Cat, urgently. She was in the tower of the castle, looking through the telescope on her watch. "I think I see something. Look, over there!"

"What is it?" asked Max.

"I'm not sure," she said. "I saw something move. It was green and shiny."

The others ran up the stairs to join her.

"I can't see anything," said Tiger. "It was probably just an insect."

"I don't think so, Tiger," said Ant. "Look at your watch!"

The red light on Tiger's watch was flashing. That could mean only one thing.

"An X-bot," said Max.

"But how did it know we were here?" asked Cat, worried.

"I don't know," said Max. "It must be one of Dr X's Spy-bots."

"Quick, let's get it!" cried Tiger.

He ran down the stairs and across to the catapult. Cat told him which way to point it. Tiger fired off one of the water balloons. It landed right on top of the X2 which fizzed and rolled over, twitching.

"Direct hit!" said Max.

They all cheered.

"But look," said Cat, "there isn't just one. There are loads of them!"

The micro-friends were very afraid now. Hundreds of X-bots were coming up out of a drain and marching across the park.

"Oh, no!" Ant groaned. "There's an army of them!"

"And they look *really* nasty," wailed Cat.

"OK," said Max, who was trying to remain calm. "We've got a choice. We can run away, or we can stay and defend our den. What do you say?"

"I don't know about you, but I'm not letting them get our castle," said Tiger, firmly.

"How about you two?" asked Max, looking at Cat and Ant.

Without hesitating, they shouted, "Stay!"

The micro-friends got ready to meet the attack.

To be continued . . .

Find out more ...

Find out what happens
next, read ...

Attack of the X-Bots!